Designer's Note:

Anyone who knows me knows that I love to crochet socks. But what quite a few people don't know about me is that I am a huge Rock n' Roll Fan. You name it... from the 1950s and Little Richard to 2000 and beyond with bands like Daughtry and Nickleback and everything in between, I truly love Rock 'n Roll.

My love of socks began about 6 years ago when I discovered my Grandmother's handwritten knit sock pattern in a box of her things. I taught myself to knit that pattern, then through trial and error over the next few months, my formulas for crocheting socks was born. It has become a crochet addiction and sock patterns just keep coming.

My love of Rock 'n Roll began in the late 1970's when I was in middle school. My parents gave me my first stereo; complete with cassette player and turntable. My 8th grade year I purchased my first record album, Journey's *Departure*, with my own money and from that point forward my love affair with music was born.

What is really little known about me, unless you knew me in the 1980s, is my love of the 1980's heavy metal music. Yes, I was a head-banger with big hair! I watched Headbanger's Ball on MTV, my favorite bands were Bon Jovi, Def Leppard, Motley Crue, AC/DC and well, you get the picture. But secretly, I loved music from all the decades, and that is where this book collides with socks.

The socks in this book feature some of my favorite Rock 'n Roll songs/bands of all time. Each one will include a little story about that song, and why I love it. Each of the designs was created using color and stitches that remind me of the song in some way. I chose yarns from two local Northwest indie yarn dyers and they hand dyed them to work with each of the songs.

I hope that you enjoy the socks and stories in this book as much as I enjoyed living and creating them!

Table of Contents

Blue Suede Shoes	3
Brown Sugar	6
Dead Heads	9
We Are The Champions	12
Born In The USA	15
Purple Rain	18
Bad Name	21
Abbreviations, Special Stitches, & Diagram Key	25

Dedication

For my husband David and my children Tyler and Cassandra... Thank you for putting up with my music and yarn fanaticism

KRW Knitwear Studio Presents
Blue Suede Shoes

Love him or hate him, no one can deny that Elvis is truly the King of Rock and Roll. I learned about Elvis from my parents, but not because they liked his music. My dad loves movies, especially OLD movies. It was watching some of the classics on TV that I discovered Elvis and his style of Rock 'n Roll.

After Elvis died in 1977, I really didn't pay much attention to the hype surrounding him. That wasn't my thing, but I still enjoyed listening to songs of his that would come up on the radio when riding with my parents.

Blue Suede Shoes socks are reminiscent of the 1950s era, adding the twist of lace cuffs and beads to make them a bit more modern. Picture these socks in a pair of Mary Jane's rocking around a soda shop dance floor.

For more information about Elvis, visit the official website at www.elvis.com.

Blue Suede Shoes

Skill Level:
Intermediate

Finished Size:
Small fits foot circumference up to 8.5 inches
Medium fits foot circumference up to 9.5 inches
Large fits foot size up to 10.5 inches
Pattern is written for size Small with [Medium, Large] in brackets.

Materials:
- Black Trillium Merilion Sock (75% Superwash Merino / 25% Nylon – 4 oz / 437 Yards)
- 1 Skein - Color: Blue Suede Shoes
- Size E (3.5 mm) Crochet Hooks or size needed for gauge
- Size 6 (1.8mm) crochet hook for beading
- Yarn Needle
- Stitch Markers

Gauge:
20 Esc = 4 inches

Pattern Notes:
- To make sure socks match, work 2 socks at once.
- Do not join rounds unless otherwise indicated
- Move up markers on each row even when not indicated. Mark the beginning of the round with a different color marker so that you can remember where you are.
- The Esc stitch in the foot creates a softer fabric to walk on and keeps sock from being stiff.
- Finished socks are smaller that actual fit so that they stretch to stay on the foot.

Directions:

Toe:
Chain 11 [14, 16]

Rnd 1: Sc in 2nd ch from hook and in each ch across, place marker in last st to mark side; working along bottom of ch, sc in each ch across to end, place unique marker in last st to mark side. (20 [26, 30] sc)

Rnd 2: ✱ Sc in each sc to one sc before marked st, 2 sc in next sc, sc in marked st, 2 sc in next sc; rep from ✱ once more. (24 [30, 34] sc)

Rnd 3: ✱ Sc in each sc to one sc before marked st, 2 sc in next sc, sc in marked st, 2 sc in next sc; rep from ✱ once more. (28 [34, 38] sc)

Rnd 4: Sc in each sc around.

Rep rows 3 and 4 until there are 36 [40, 44] sc around. Remove markers.

Foot
Rnd 1: Esc in each st around. (36 [40, 44] Esc)

Rep Rnd 1 until foot is 3 inches shorter than measured foot length.

Gusset:
Lay sock flat so that toe is flat at the foundation chain. Work Esc until you reach one side. Place markers at either side so that there are 17 [19, 21] stitches between the markers on each side.

Rnd 1: Esc in marked stitch, 2 Esc in next Esc, Esc in each st to 1 stitch before next marker, 2 Esc in next Esc, Esc in marked stitch and in each stitch to end. (38 [42, 46] Esc)

Rnds 2-8: Rep Rnd 1 seven times. (52 [56, 60] Esc at end of Rnd 8)

Heel Turn:
Row 1: Esc in next 9 esc, sc in next 8 [10, 12] Esc, sl st in next Esc, turn. (8 [10, 12] sc)

Row 2: Sc in next sc, 2 sc in next sc, sc in next 4 [6, 8] sc, 2 sc in next sc, sc in last sc, sl st in next Esc, turn. (10 [12, 14] sc)

Row 3: Sc in each sc across, sl st in next Esc, turn.

Row 4: Sc in next sc, 2 sc in next 2 sc, sc in next 4 [6, 8] sc, 2 sc in next 2 sc, sc in last sc, sl st in next Esc, turn. (14 [16, 18] sc)

Row 5: Rep row 3.

Row 6: Sc in next sc, 2 sc in next 2 sc, sc in next 8 [10, 12] sc, 2 sc in next 2 sc, sc in last sc, sl st in next Esc, turn. (18 [20, 22] sc)

Heel Flap:
Row 7: Sc in each sc across, sl st in next Esc, turn.

Rows 8-27: Rep Row 7.

Leg:
Rnd 1-5: Esc in each st around. At end of rnd 5, join with sl st in first sc. (36 [40, 44] Esc)

Cuff:
Rnd 1: With smaller hook and wrong side of sock facing you, Esc in back loop of each Esc around. (36 [40, 44] Esc)

Rnd 2: Esc in each Esc around.

Rnd 3: Sc in next Esc, * ch 1, Bch, ch 2, Bch, ch 1, sk next Esc, sc in next Esc; rep from * to last Esc, ch 1, Bch, Bdc in first sc of rnd. (18 [20, 22] ch-5 bead loops loops)

Rnd 4: [Ch 1, Bch, ch 3, bch, ch1, sc in next ch-5 loop] across to last ch-5 loop, ch 1, Bch, ch 1, Bdc in dc of last rnd. (18 [20, 22] ch-5 bead loops)

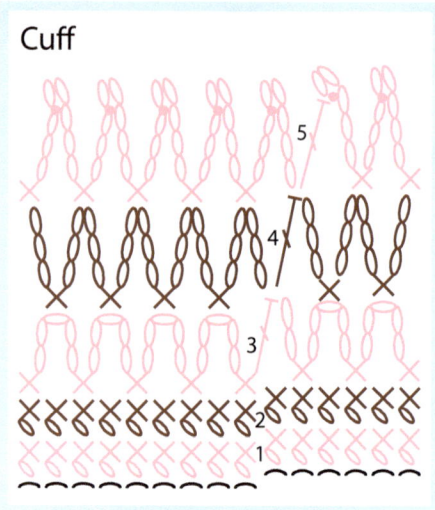

Cuff

Rnd 5: [Ch 4, Bch, ch 1, sl st in 3rd ch from hook (picot made), ch 3, sc in next ch-6 loop] to last ch-6 loop; Ch 4, Bch, ch 1, sl st in 3rd ch from hook (picot made), dc in dc of last rnd. (18 [20, 22] beaded picot loops).

Fasten off and weave in all ends

Brown Sugar

If I am going to be honest, I think started to listen to The Rolling Stones as a teenager to spite my parents!

I remember my father telling me when I first got my Stereo way back in the late 1970s that he didn't mind rock music, except The Rolling Stones!

Tattoo You is the only actual album I purchased that the Stones produced, though I had 45s (singles for those of you who are not of the vinyl era of music) of many of their hits. To me, Mick Jagger and company are truly the epitome of come backs and staying power. This year marks 50 years of the Stones, and even nay-sayers like my dad have to admit that is pretty darn amazing!

Brown Sugar socks were designed around the very first Rolling Stones song I remember hearing. The color and the style are a bit eclectic. However, I feel that they will become a true classic sock, just like their namesake song!

For more information on The Rolling Stones, visit their website at www.rollingstones.com

Brown Sugar

Skill Level:
Intermediate

Finished Size:
Small fits foot circumference up to 8.5 inches
Medium fits foot circumference up to 9.5 inches
Large fits foot circumference up to 10.5 inches
Pattern is written for size Small with [Medium, Large] in brackets.

Materials:
- Black Trillium Bison Sock (90% Superwash Merino / 10% American Buffalo Down – 4 oz / 400 Yards)
- 1 Skein - Color: Butterbeer
- Size E (3.5 mm) Crochet Hook or size needed for gauge
- Yarn Needle
- Stitch Markers

Gauge:
20 esc = 4 inches

Pattern Notes:
- To make sure socks match, work 2 socks at once.
- Do not join rounds unless otherwise indicated.
- Move up markers on each row even when not indicated.
- Mark the beginning of the round with a different color marker so that you can remember where you are.
- Finished socks are smaller that actual fit so that they stretch to stay on the foot.

Directions:

Toe:
Chain 11 [14, 16]
Rnd 1: Sc in 2nd ch from hook and in each ch across, place marker in last st to mark side; working along bottom of ch, sc in each ch across to end, place unique marker in last st to mark side. (20 [26, 30] sc)

Rnd 2: ✻ Sc in each sc to one sc before marked st, 2 sc in next sc, sc in marked st, 2 sc in next sc; rep from ✻ once more. (24 [30, 34] sc)

Rnd 3: ✻ Sc in each sc to one sc before marked st, 2 sc in next sc, sc in marked st, 2 sc in next sc; rep from ✻ once more. (28 [34, 38] sc)

Rnd 4: Sc in each sc around.

Rep rows 3 and 4 until there are 36 [42, 46] sc around.

Next row: (*Sets up stitches for pattern*) Sc in each st to the next marker; sc in marked st and in next st. Remove markers.

Foot:
Rnd 1 (RS): Sc in next st, PM in this st for beg of rnd marker, ✻ ch 3, dc4tog over next 4 sts, ch 1, sc in next st; rep from ✻ around ending with sl st in beg sc, ch 1, turn. (7 [8, 9] dc4tog)

Rnd 2: ✻ Sc in top of next dc4tog, ch 3, dc4tog in next ch-3 sp, ch 1; rep from ✻ around ending with sl st in beg sc, ch 1, turn.

Rep Rnd 2 until foot measures approx. 3 inches short of length of foot, ending with ws rnd.

Short Row Heel:
Row 1: Sc in next 21 [21, 26] sts/chs, ch 1, turn. leaving remaining sts unworked.

Row 2: Sc in each sc across, ch 1, turn.

Row 3: Sc in each sc across to last st, leave last st unworked, ch 1, turn.

Rows 4-14: Rep Row 3 until 9 [9, 13] sts remain.

Row 15: Sc in each sc across, ch 1, turn.

Row 16: Sc in each sc across, sc in unworked st in row below closest to current row, sl st in side of that row, turn. (10 [10, 14] sc)

Row 17: Sk sl st, sc in each sc across, sc in unworked st in row below closest to current row, sl st in side of that row, turn. (11 [11, 15] sc)

Row 18-27: Rep row 17. At end of Row 27, do not turn. (21 [21, 26] sc)

Leg:
Rnd 1: Sc in next st, ✱ ch 3, dc4tog over next 4 sts, ch 1, sc in next st; rep from ✱ around, join with sl st in first sc. Turn.

Rnd 2 (WS): Ch 3, dc4tog in next ch-3 sp, ch 1, ✱ sc in next dc4tog, ch 3, dc4tog in next ch-3 sp, ch 1; rep from ✱ 2 [3, 4] times, sc in 1st sc of heel; + ch 3, dc4tog over next 4 sts, ch 1, sc in next st; rep from + 3 [3, 4] times, ending with sl st in top of beg ch-3, ch 1, turn. (7 [8, 9] dc4tog)

Rnd 3: ✱ Sc in top of next dc4tog, ch 3, dc4tog in next ch-3 sp, ch 1; rep from ✱ around ending with sl st in beg sc, ch 1, turn.

Rep rnd 3 until leg measures approx. 4 inches ending with ws rnd.

Cuff:
Rnd 1: Ch 3, evenly space 36 [40, 46] dc around; join with sl st in 3rd ch of beg ch 3. (36 [40, 46] dc)

Rnd 2: Ch 3, FPdc in next dc, * dc in next dc, FPdc in next dc; rep from * around; Join with sl st in 3rd ch of beg ch 3. (18 [20, 23] FPdc, 18 [20,23] dc)

Rnd 3: Ch 3, FPdc in next FPdc, * dc in next dc, FPdc in next FPdc; rep from * around; Join with sl st in 3rd ch of beg ch 3. (18 [20, 23] FPdc, 18 [20,23] dc)
Rnd 4: Rep Rnd 3. Fasten off

Weave in all ends.

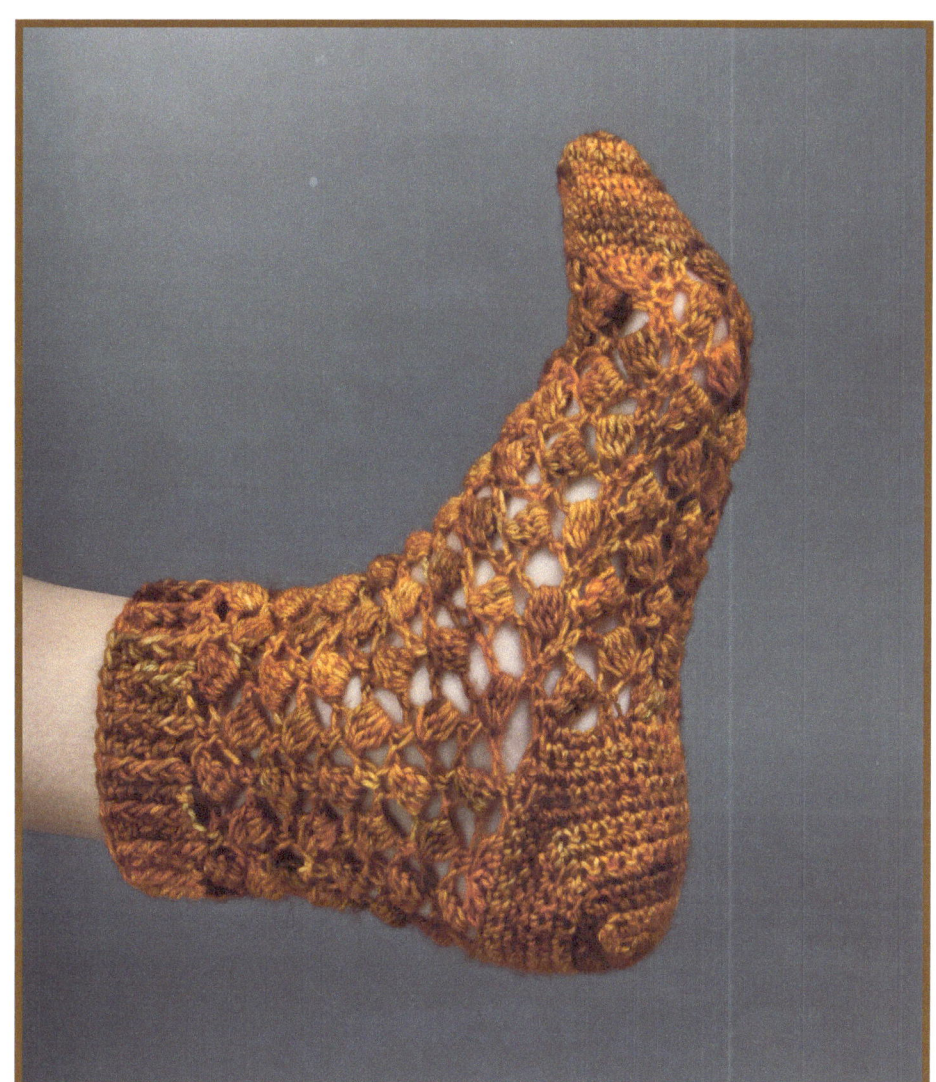

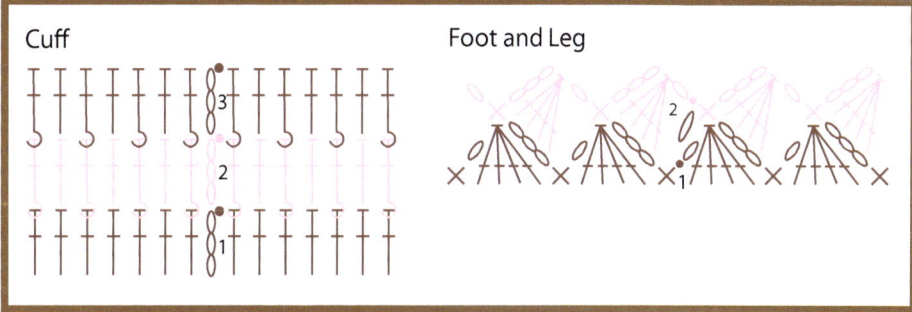

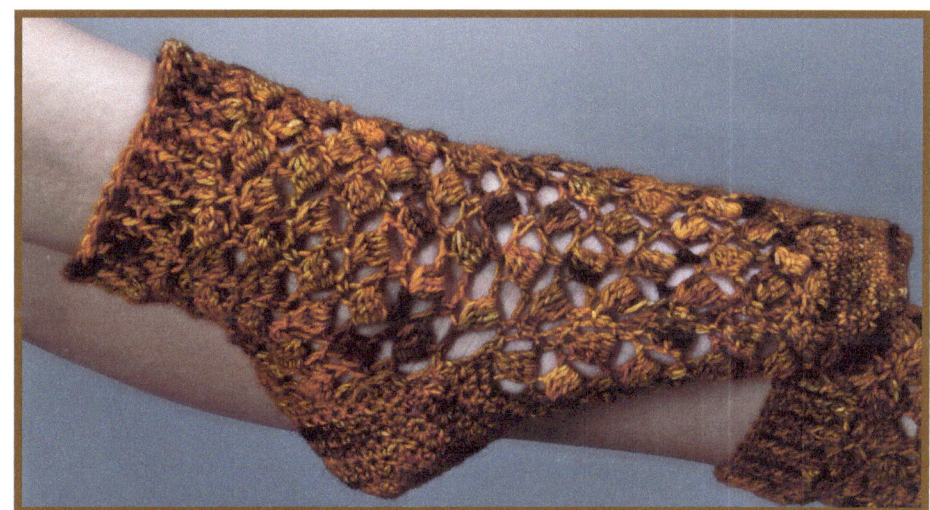

Dead Heads

Skill Level:
Intermediate

Finished Size:
Small fits foot circumference up to 8.5 inches
Medium fits foot circumference up to 9.5 inches
Large fits foot circumference up to 10.5 inches
Pattern is written for size Small with [Medium, Large] in brackets.

Materials:
- Knitted Wit Fingering (100% Superwash Merino – 3.5 oz / 400 Yards)
- 1 Skein - Color: Dead Head
- Size D (3.25 mm) and Size E (3.5 mm) Crochet Hooks or size needed for gauge
- Yarn Needle
- Stitch Markers

Gauge:
20 esc = 4 inches

Pattern Notes:
- To make sure socks match, work 2 socks at once.
- Do not join rounds unless otherwise indicated.
- Move up markers on each row even when not indicated.
- Mark the beginning of the round with a different color marker so that you can remember where you are.
- The Esc stitch in the foot creates a softer fabric to walk on and keeps sock from being stiff.
- Finished socks are smaller than actual fit so that they stretch to stay on the foot.

Dead Heads

These socks are designed more for the followers of the Grateful Dead, rather than any one song. Back in high school, many of my friends were "dead heads" and tie dye was a constant visual of where they would hang out. In the 1990s, my husband became a huge fan of Jerry Garcia ties so in a way this pattern is reflects him too.

The Dead Heads socks are designed with the Catherine Wheel, which gives a bit of that tie-dyed look to the fabric using wonderfully bright colored yarn in traditional tie-dye colors

For more information on the Grateful Dead, visit their website at www.dead.net

Directions:

Cuff:
Rnd 1: With Smaller hook, dcf 39 [49, 59] times, join with sl st to top of beg ch, 3. (40 [50, 60] dcf)

NOTE: *Beg ch-3 counts as the first stitch unless otherwise noted.*

Rnd 2: Ch 3, FPdc around next dc, ✱dc in next dc, FPdc around next dc; rep from ✱ around, join with sl st in 3rd ch of beg ch 3. (20 [25, 30] dc, 20 [25, 30] FPdc)

Rnd 3: Ch 3, FPdc around next FPdc, ✱dc in next dc, FPdc around next FPdc; rep from ✱ around, join with sl st in 3rd ch of beg ch 3. (20 [25, 30] dc, 20 [25, 30] FPdc)

Leg:
NOTES:
Mark 1st stitch of rnd now and throughout unless otherwise indicated.

Rnd 1: Switching to larger hook, Esc in each st around; join with sl st in first Esc. (40 [50, 60] esc)

Rnd 2: Ch 3 (counts as first dc), 3 dc in same Esc as join, skip 3 Esc, sc in each of next 3 Esc, skip 3 Esc, ✱ 7 dc in next Esc, skip 3 Esc, sc in each of next 3 Esc, skip 3 Esc; rep from ✱ 2 [3, 4] times, 3 dc in same st as join of previous rnd, join to top of ch 3 with sl st. (4 [5, 6] half wheels)

Rnd 3: Ch 1, sc in same st as join and in next st, ✱ ch 3, CL over next 7 sts, ch 3, sc in each of next 3 sts; rep from ✱ 2 [3, 4] times, ch 3, CL over next 7 sts, ch 3, sc in last st, join with sl st in 1st sc.

Rnd 4: Ch 1, sc in same sc as join and in next sc, skip 3 ch, 7 dc into loop that closed CL, ✱ skip 3 ch, sc in each of next 3 sc, skip 3 ch, 7 dc into loop that closed CL; rep from ✱ 2 [3, 4] times, skip 3 ch, sc in last st, join with sl st in 1st sc.

Rnd 5: Ch 3 (counts as first dc), CL over next 3 sts, ✱ ch 3, sc in each of next 3 sts, ch 3, CL over next 7 sts; rep from ✱ 2 [3, 4] times, ch 3, sc in each of next 3 sts, ch 3, CL over next 4 sts, join with sl st in loop that closed CL.

Rnd 6: Ch 3 (counts as first dc), 3 dc in same st, ✱ skip 3 ch, sc in each of next 3 sc, skip 3 ch, 7 dc into loop that closed CL; rep from ✱ 11 times, skip 3 ch, sc in each of next 3 sc, skip 3 ch, 3 dc into loop that closed CL, join with sl st in beg ch-3.

Rnds 7 – 14: Rep rnds 3-6 twice more.

Rnd 15: Esc in each st and ch around. (40 [50, 60] esc)

Heel Flap:
NOTE: *For the Heel, you are now working in Rows instead of Rnds.*

Row 1 (RS): Evenly space 20 [25, 30] sc across, leaving the remaining ½ of the sock unworked. Ch 1, turn.

Row 2: Sc in each sc across; ch 1, turn. (20 [25, 30] sc) Repeat Row 2 until heel flap measures 2 ¾ inches (approximately 20 rows), ending on a WS row.

Heel Turn:
Row 1 (RS): Sc in next sc, Sc2tog twice, sc in next 10 [15, 20] sc, sc2tog twice, sc in last sc; ch 1, turn. (16 [21, 26] sts)

Row 2: Sc in each st across; ch 1, turn.

Row 3: Sc in next sc, sc2tog twice, sc in next 6 [11, 16] sc, sc2tog twice, sc in last sc; ch 1, turn. (12 [17, 22] sts)

Row 4: Rep Row 2.

Row 5: Sc in next sc, sc2tog, sc in next 6 [11, 16] sc, sc2tog, sc in last sc; ch 1, turn. (10 [15, 20] sts)

Gusset:
Rnd 1 (RS): Evenly place 13 sc along right edge of Heel Turn/Flap, PM (for gusset) in last sc worked, sc in each of unworked Esc and , evenly space 13 sc along left side of Heel Flap/Turn, PM (for gusset) in first sc worked. Do not work sts along top of heel turn. (56 [66, 76] sc around including unworked sts of heel)

NOTE: Place unique marker in first st or rnd from this point forward unless otherwise stated.

Rnd 2: Esc in each st to 2 st before first gusset marker, sc2tog, Esc in marked sc, Esc in each st to next marker, Esc in marked st, sc2tog, Esc in each sc to end.

Rep Rnd 2 until there are 36 [40, 44] Esc around. Remove Gusset Markers

Foot:
Rnd 1: Esc in each st around.

Rep Rnd 1 until foot is 2 inches shorter than length of foot.
Toe:

Rnd 1: Sc in each sc around. Fold Sock, making sure that the heel is centered to the back and place markers at each side edge. There should be 17 [19, 21] sts between each marker on either side. If you are not starting the next st in marked stitch, either sc to next marked st, or pull out to previous marked stitch.

Rnd 2: Sc in each sc to 2 sc before next marked sc, sc2tog, sc in marked sc, sc2tog, sc in each sc to 2 sc prior to next marker, sc2tog, sc in next marked sc, sc2tog, sc in each sc to beg of rnd marker.

Rnd 3: Sc in each sc around.

Rep Rnds 2 and 3 until 20 (24, 28) sc left. Join with sl st to 1st sc. Fasten off.

Turning Sock inside out, whipstitch toe together.

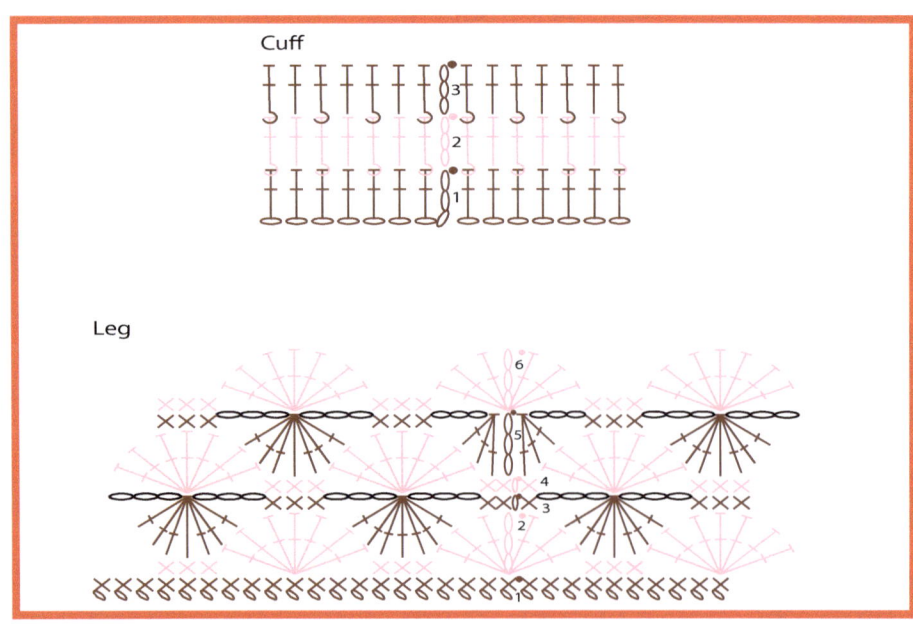

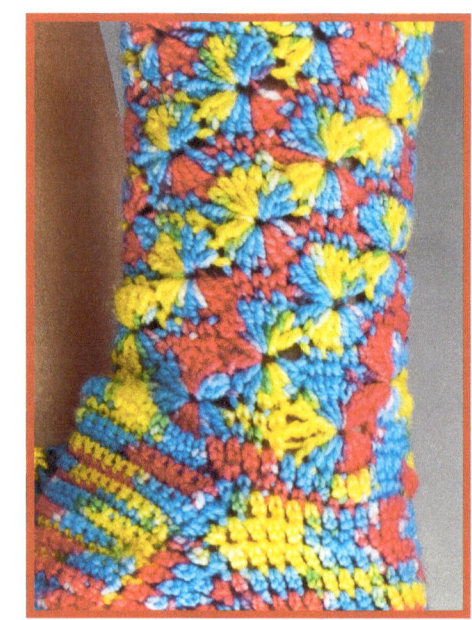

Queen is one of the very first rock bands I listened to. Freddie Mercury will always live in my heart as one of the greatest singers in history. It was a very sad day when his light was taken from this world into the next.

"We Will Rock You" & "We Are The Champions" are another two songs that seem to evoke my emotions. I remember driving to volleyball games and listening to these songs, belting them out with my teammates in preparation to win our matches. Everytime they are played at a professional ball game, it still floors me when you can hear almost the entire crowd sing these songs.

We Are The Champions socks were designed with the sports theme in mind. As 2012 is an Olympics year the colors of Gold, Silver and Bronze were used in the yarn. Tube sock style, they are simple socks to make, with just a hint of looped cables signifying team-work.

For more information about Queen, visit their website at: www.queenonline.com

We Are The Champions

Skill Level:
Intermediate

Finished Size:
Small fits foot circumference up to 8.5 inches
Medium fits foot circumference up to 9.5 inches
Large fits foot circumference up to 10.5 inches
Pattern is written for size Small with [Medium, Large] in brackets.

Materials:
- Knitted Wit Cashy Wool (70% Superwash Merino / 20% Cashmere / 10% Nylon – 4 oz / 400 Yards)
- 1 Skein - Color: Going the Distance
- Size E (3.5 mm) Crochet Hooks or size needed for gauge
- Yarn Needle
- Stitch Markers
- Thread weight elastic cord (optional)

Gauge:
20 esc = 4 inches

Pattern Notes:
- To make sure socks match, work 2 socks at once.
- Do not join rounds unless otherwise indicated.
- Move up markers on each row even when not indicated.
- Mark the beginning of the round with a different color marker so that you can remember where you are.
- The Esc stitch in the foot creates a softer fabric to walk on and keeps sock from being stiff.
- Finished socks are smaller than actual fit so that they stretch to stay on the foot.

DIRECTIONS:

Toe:
Chain 11 [14, 16]

Rnd 1: Sc in 2nd ch from hook and in each ch across, place marker in last st to mark side; working along bottom of ch, sc in each ch across to end, place unique marker in last st to mark side. (20 [26, 30] sc)

Rnd 2: ✱ Sc in each sc to one sc before marked st, 2 sc in next sc, sc in marked st, 2 sc in next sc; rep from ✱ once more. (24 [30, 34] sc)

Rnd 3: ✱ Sc in each sc to one sc before marked st, 2 sc in next sc, sc in marked st, 2 sc in next sc; rep from ✱ once more. (28 [34, 38] sc)

Rnd 4: Sc in each sc around.

Rep rows 3 and 4 until there are 36 [42, 46] sc around.

Next row: (*Sets up stitches for Cabling*) Sc in each st to the next marker; sc in marked st and in next st. Remove marker.

Leg:
Rnd 1-2: Esc in each st around. (36 [42, 46] Esc)

Rnd 3: Esc in next 3 [5, 6] st, (FPdc around next stitch 2 rows below) twice, Esc in next 8 sts, (FPdc around next stitch 2 rows below) twice, esc in last 21 [25, 28] sts. (4 FPdc, 32 [38, 42] Esc)

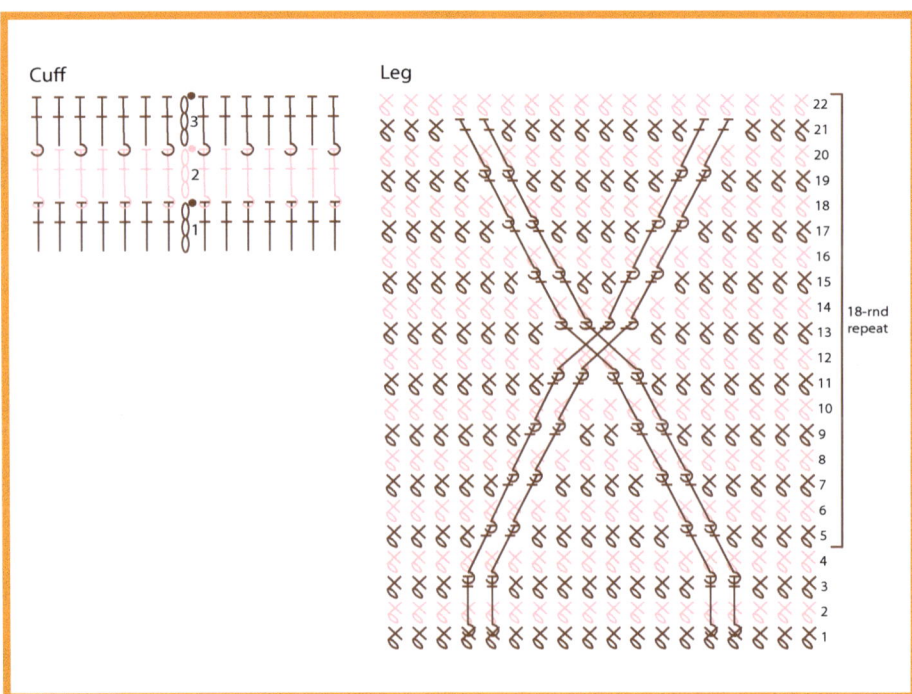

Rnd 4 (and all even rnds): Esc in each st around. (36 [42, 46] Esc)

Rnd 5: Esc in next 4 [6, 7] st, (FPdc around FPdc 2 rows below) twice, Esc in next 6 sts, (FPdc around FPdc 2 rows below) twice, Esc in last 22 [26, 29] sts. (4 FPdc, 32 [38, 42] Esc)

Rnd 7: Esc in next 5 [7, 8] st, (FPdc around FPdc 2 rows below) twice, Esc in next 4 sts, (FPdc around FPdc 2 rows below) twice, Esc in last 23 [27, 30] sts. (4 FPdc, 32 [38, 42] Esc)

Rnd 9: Esc in next 6 [8, 9] st, (FPdc around FPdc 2 rows below) twice, Esc in next 2 sts, (FPdc around FPdc 2 rows below) twice, Esc in last 24 [28, 31] sts. (4 FPdc, 32 [38, 42] Esc)

Rnd 11: Esc in next 7 [9, 10] st, (FPdc around FPdc 2 rows below) four times, Esc in last 25 [29, 32] sts. (4 FPdc, 32 [38, 42] Esc)

Rnd 13: Esc in next 7 [9, 10] st, skip 2 FPdc, FPdc around FPdc 2 rows below, working around skipped FPdc, FPdc around FPdc 2 rows below, Esc in last 25 [29, 32] sts. (4 FPdc, 32 [38, 42] Esc)

Rnd 15: Rep Row 9

Rnd 17: Rep Rnd 7

Rnd 19: Rep Rnd 5

Rnd 21: Rep Rnd 3

Rnd 22: Rep Rnd 4.

Rnds 23-76: Rep Rnds 5-22 three times more.

Cuff:

Rnd 1: Ch 3, dc in each st around; join with sl st in 3rd ch of beg ch 3. (36 [42, 46] dc)

Rnd 2: Ch 3, FPdc around next dc, ✽ dc in next dc, FPdc around next dc; rep from ✽ around; join with sl st in 3rd ch of beg ch 3. (18 [21, 23] FPdc, 18 [21, 23] dc)

Rnd 3: Ch 3, FPdc around next FPdc, ✽ dc in next dc, FPdc around next FPdc; rep from ✽ around; join with sl st in 3rd ch of beg ch 3. (18 [21, 23] FPdc, 18 [21, 23] dc)

Rnd 4: Rep Rnd 3. Fasten off. Weave in all ends.

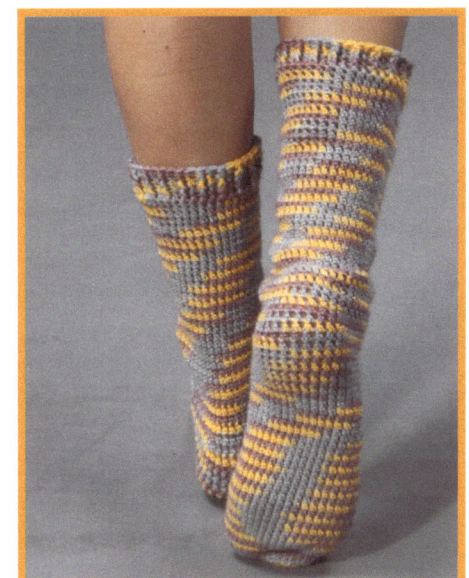

Born In The USA

Skill Level:
Intermediate

Finished Size:
Small fits foot circumference up to 8.5 inches
Medium fits foot circumference up to 9.5 inches
Large fits foot circumference up to 10.5 inches
Pattern is written for size Small with [Medium, Large] in brackets.

Materials:
- Knitted Wit Fingering (100% Superwash Merino – 3.5 oz / 400 Yards)
- 1 Skein - Color: Born Free
- Size D (3.25 mm) and Size E (3.5 mm) Crochet Hooks or size needed for gauge
- Yarn Needle
- Stitch Markers

Gauge:
20 Esc = 4 inches

Pattern Notes:
- To make sure socks match, work 2 socks at once.
- Do not join rounds unless otherwise indicated.
- Move up markers on each row even when not indicated.
- Mark the beginning of the round with a different color marker so that you can remember where you are.
- The Esc stitch in the foot creates a softer fabric to walk on and keeps sock from being stiff.
- Finished socks are smaller than actual fit so that they stretch to stay on the foot.

BORN IN THE USA

I discovered Bruce Springsteen in 1984 when the title song of this highly acclaimed album was released. Over the years, I have learned to appreciate his music from previous and future albums, but nothing will replace the *Born In The USA* album in my heart when it comes to Bruce.

The song, "Born in the USA" always reminded me of my pride in being an American. The down to earth music video that hails Bruce an approachable musician has to be one of my favorites for the 1980s.

The Born in the USA socks were designed with this in mind. Red white and blue yarn, crocheted in a type of "wave" pattern, giving a nod to America's heartland.

For more information about Bruce Springsteen, visit his website at http://brucespringsteen.net

DIRECTIONS:

Cuff:
Rnd 1: With Smaller hook, dcf 35 [39, 43] times, join with sl st to top of beg ch 3. (36 [40, 44] dcf)
NOTE: Beg ch-3 counts as the first stitch unless otherwise noted.

Rnd 2: Ch 3, FPdc around next dc, ✱dc in next dc, FPdc around next dc; rep from ✱ around, join with sl st in 3rd ch of beg ch 3. (18 [20, 22] dc, 18 [20, 22] FPdc)

Rnd 3: Ch 3, FPdc around next FPdc, ✱dc in next dc, FPdc around next FPdc; rep from ✱ around, join with sl st in 3rd ch of beg ch 3. (18 [20, 22] dc, 18 [20, 22] FPdc)

Leg:
NOTE: Mark 1st stitch of rnd now and throughout unless otherwise indicated.

Rnd 1: Switching to larger hook, ch 1, ✱ sc in next st, ch 1, sk 1 st; rep from ✱ around, join with sl st in first sc. (18 [20, 22] sc, 18 [20, 22] ch-1 sps)

Rnd 2: Ch 3, dc in next ch-1 sp (counts as 1st dc2tog), ch 1,✱ dc2tog inserting hook into same sp as previous st for 1st leg and into next ch-1 sp for 2nd leg, ch 1; rep from ✱ around, join with sl st in top of first dc. (18 [20, 22] dc2tog, 18 [20, 22] ch-1 sps)

Rnd 3: Ch 1, ✱ sc in next ch-1 sp, ch 1, sk 1 sc; rep from ✱ around, join with sl st in first sc. (18 [20, 22] sc, 18 [20, 22] ch-1 sps)

Rnds 4 -11: Rep Rnds 2-3 four times

Rnd 12: Esc in each st and ch-1 sp around.

Heel Flap:
NOTE: For the Heel, you are now working in Rows instead of Rnds.

Row 1 (RS): Evenly space 18 [20, 22] sc across, leaving the remaining ½ of the sock unworked. Ch 1, turn.

Row 2: Sc in each sc across; ch 1, turn. (18 [20, 22] sc)

Row 3: Sc in first sc, ✱ sc in next sc 2 rows below, sc in next sc; rep from ✱ across, ch 1, turn.

Repeat Rows 2 and 3 until heel flap measures 2 ¾ inches (approximately 20 rows), ending with Row 2.

Heel Turn:
Row 1 (RS): Sc in next sc, sc2tog twice, sc in next 8 [10, 12] sc, sc2tog twice, sc in last sc; ch 1, turn. 14 [16, 18] sts)

Row 2: Sc in each st across; ch 1, turn.

Row 3: Sc in next sc, sc2tog twice, sc in next 4 [6, 8] sc, sc2tog twice, sc in last sc; ch 1, turn. (10 [12, 14] sts)

Row 4: Rep Row 2.

Row 5: Sc in next sc, sc2tog, sc in next 4 [6, 8] sc, sc2tog, sc in last sc; ch 1, do not turn. (8 [10, 12] sts)

Gusset:
Rnd 1 (RS): Evenly place 13 sc along right edge of Heel Turn/Flap, PM (for gusset) in last sc worked, sc in each of unworked Esc, evenly space 13 sc along left side of Heel Flap/Turn, PM (for gusset) in first sc worked. Do not work sts along top of heel turn. (52 [56, 60] sc around including unworked sts of heel)

NOTE: *Place unique marker in first st or rnd from this point forward unless otherwise stated.*

Rnd 2: Esc in each st to 2 st before first gusset marker, sc2tog, Esc in marked sc, Esc in each st to next marker, Esc in marked st, sc2tog, Esc in each sc to end.

Rep Rnd 2 until there are 36 [40, 44] Esc around. Remove Gusset Markers

Foot:
Rnd 1: Esc in each st around.

Rep Rnd 1 until foot is 2 inches shorter than length of foot.

Toe:
Rnd 1: Sc in each sc around.

Fold Sock, making sure that the heel is centered to the back and place markers at each side edge. There should be 17 [19, 21] sts between each marker on either side. If you are not starting the next st in marked stitch, either sc to next marked st, or pull out to previous marked stitch.

Rnd 2: Sc in each sc to 2 sc before next marked sc, sc2tog, sc in marked sc, sc2tog, sc in each sc to 2 sc prior to next marker, sc2tog, sc in next marked sc, sc2tog, sc in each sc to beg of rnd marker.

Rnd 3: Sc in each sc around.

Rep Rnds 2 and 3 until 20 (24, 28) sc left. Join with sl st to 1st sc. Fasten off.

Turning Sock inside out, whipstitch toe together.

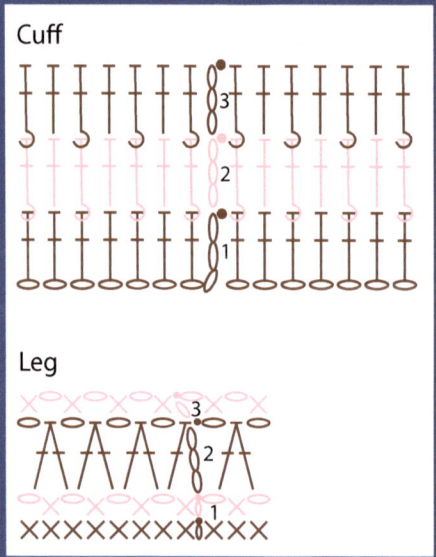

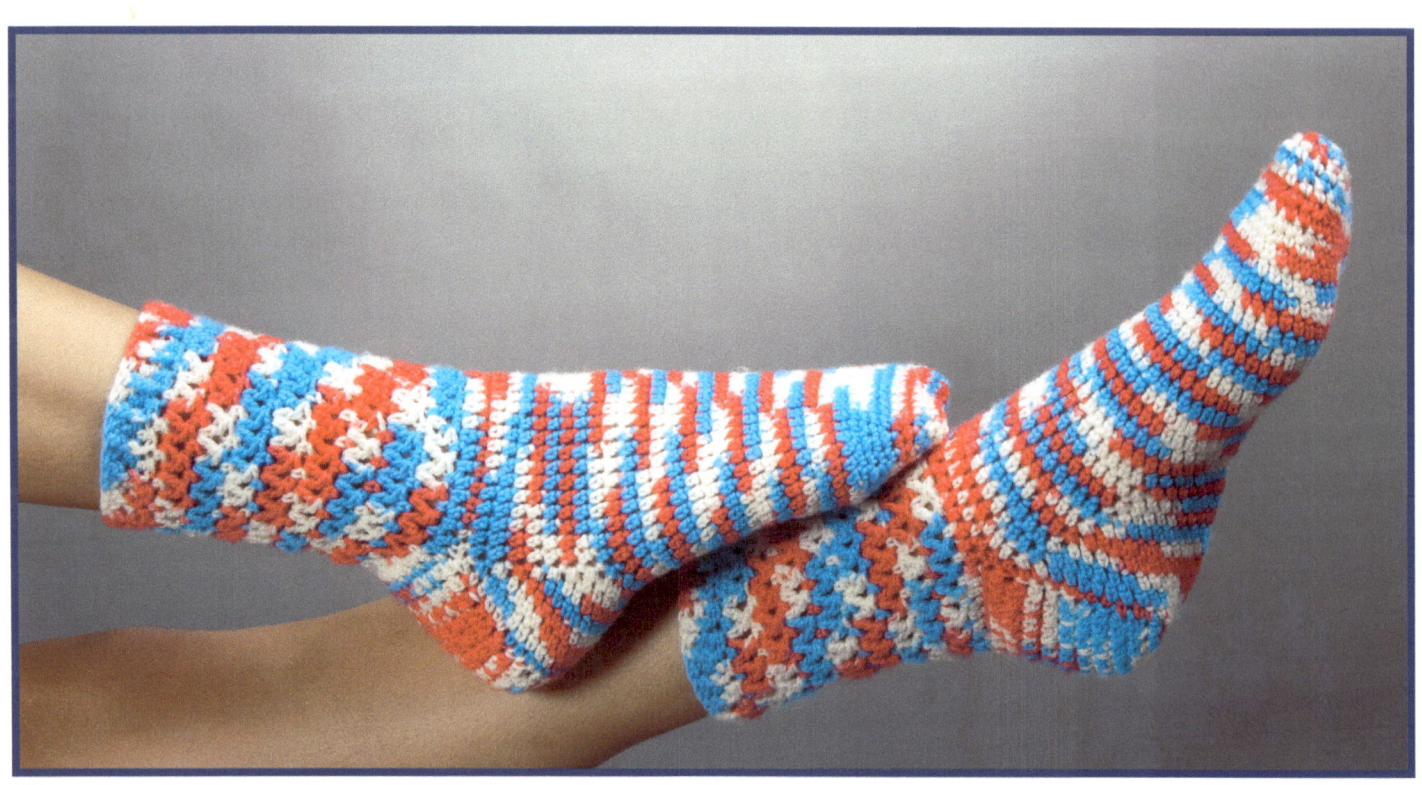

No matter how I look at it, Prince and his music are all about a feeling and a vibe of my teenage years. When the *Purple Rain* movie and album were released, it took hold through my entire group of friends. "Let's Go Crazy" was almost an anthem for my high school class. Hearing the words "Dearly Beloved" evoke an urge to run out to the nearest dance floor and rock out to any Prince song.

The Purple Rain socks were designed to inspire that same feeling. The heliotrope – purple color along with the spike stitches evokes that feeling of Rock 'n Roll edgy-ness from the era of which they are named for. I'm taking my pair to the nearest dance club…

For more information about Prince, visit his unofficial fan website at http://www.prince.org.

Purple Rain

Skill Level:
Intermediate

Finished Size:
Small fits foot circumference up to 8.5 inches
Medium fits foot circumference up to 9.5 inches
Large fits foot circumference up to 10.5 inches
Pattern is written for size Small with [Medium, Large] in brackets.

Materials:
- Black Trillium Bison Sock (90% Superwash Merino / 10% American Buffalo down – 4 oz / 400 Yards)
- 1 Skein - Color: Helotrope
- Size E (3.5 mm) Crochet Hooks or size needed for gauge
- Yarn Needle
- Stitch Markers

Gauge:
20 esc = 4 inches

Pattern Notes:
- To make sure socks match, work 2 socks at once.
- Do not join rounds unless otherwise indicated.
- Move up markers on each row even when not indicated.
- Mark the beginning of the round with a different color marker so that you can remember where you are.
- The Esc stitch in the foot creates a softer fabric to walk on and keeps sock from being stiff.
- Finished socks are smaller than actual fit so that they stretch to stay on the foot.

Directions:

Toe:
Chain 11 [14, 16]

Rnd 1: Sc in 2nd ch from hook and in each ch across, place marker in last st to mark side; working along bottom of ch, sc in each ch across to end, place unique marker in last st to mark side. (20 [26, 30] sc)

Rnd 2: ✱ Sc in each sc to one sc before marked st, 2 sc in next sc, sc in marked st, 2 sc in next sc; rep from ✱ once more. (24 [30, 34] sc)

Rnd 3: ✱ Sc in each sc to one sc before marked st, 2 sc in next sc, sc in marked st, 2 sc in next sc; rep from ✱ once more. (28 [34, 38] sc)

Rnd 4: Sc in each sc around.

Rep rows 3 and 4 until there are 36 [42, 46] sc around. Remove markers.

Foot:
Rnd 1: Esc in each st around. (36 [42, 46] Esc)
Rep Rnd 1 until foot is 3 inches shorter than measured foot length.

Gusset:
Lay sock flat so that toe is flat at the foundation chain. Work Esc until you reach one side. Place markers at either side so that there are 17 [20, 22] stitches between the markers on each side.

Rnd 1: Esc in marked stitch, 2 Esc in next Esc, Esc in each st to 1 stitch before next marker, 2 Esc in next Esc, Esc in marked stitch and in each stitch to end. (38 [44, 48] Esc)

Rnds 2-8: Rep Rnd 1 seven times. (52 [58, 62] Esc at end of Rnd 8)

Heel Turn:
Row 1: Esc in next 9 [9, 9] Esc, sc in next 8 [10, 12] Esc sl st in next Esc, turn. (8 [10, 12] sc)

Row 2: Sc in next sc, 2 sc in next sc, sc in next 4 [6, 8] sc, 2 sc in next sc, sc in last sc, sl st in next Esc, turn. (10 [12, 14] sc)

Row 3: Sc in each sc across, sl st in next Esc, turn.

Row 4: Sc in next sc, 2 sc in next 2 sc, sc in next 4 [6, 8] sc, 2 sc in next 2 sc, sc in last sc, sl st in next Esc, turn. (14 [16, 18] sc)

Row 5: Rep row 3.

Row 6: Sc in next sc, 2 sc in next 2sc, sc in next 8 [10, 12] sc, 2 sc in next sc, sc in last sc, sl st in next Esc, turn. (18 [20, 22] sc)

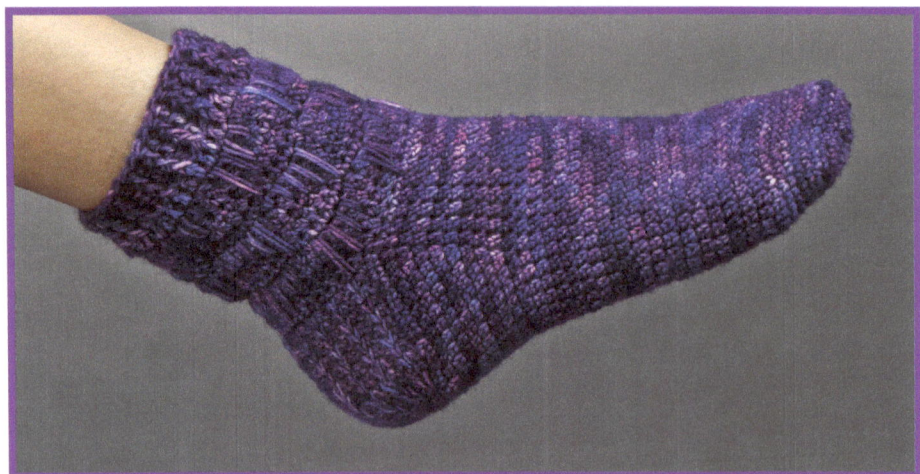

Heel Flap:

Row 7: Sc in next sc, * sc in next sc 2 rows below, sc in next sc; rep from * across all sc, sl st in next Esc, turn.

Row 8: Sc in each sc across, sl st in next Esc, turn.

Rows 9-24: Rep rows 7 and 8 eight times.

Row 25: Rep row 7.

Leg:

Rnd 1: Evenly space 36 [42, 48] Esc around. Join with sl st to top of first Esc, ch 1, turn.

Rnd 2: Esc in each Esc, join with sl st at top of 1st Esc, ch 1, turn.

Rnds 3-5: Rep Rnd 2.

Rnd 6: *Sc in next st, Ssc1 over next st, Ssc2 over next st, Ssc3 over next st, Ssc4 over next st, Ssc5 over next st, sc in next st; rep from * around ending with sl st in first sc; ch 1, turn.

Rnds 7-11: Rep Rnd 2

Rnd 12: *Sc in next st, Ssc5 over next st, Ssc4 over next st, Ssc3 over next st, Ssc2 over next st, Ssc1 over next st, sc in next st; rep from * around ending with sl st in first sc; ch 1, turn.

Rnds 13-17: Rep Rnd 2.

Rnd 18: Rep Rnd 6. Ch 3, turn at end of rnd.

Cuff:

Rnd 1: Dc in next st and in each st around. (36 [42, 48] dc)

Rnd 2: Ch 3, FPdc around next dc, * dc in next dc, FPdc around next dc; rep from * around; Join with sl st in 3rd ch of beg ch 3. (18 [21, 24] FPdc, 18 [21, 24] dc)

Rnd 3: Ch 3, FPdc around next FPdc, * dc in next dc, FPdc around next FPdc; rep from * around; Join with sl st in 3rd ch of beg ch 3. (18 [21, 24] FPdc, 18 [21, 24] dc)

Rnd 4: Rep Rnd 3. Fasten off

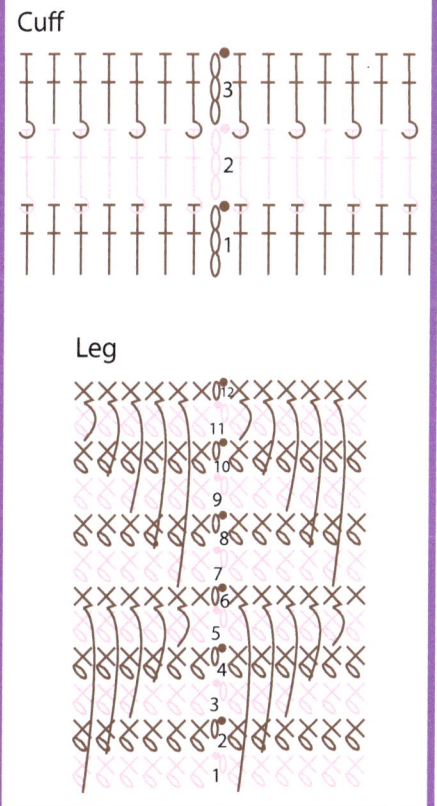

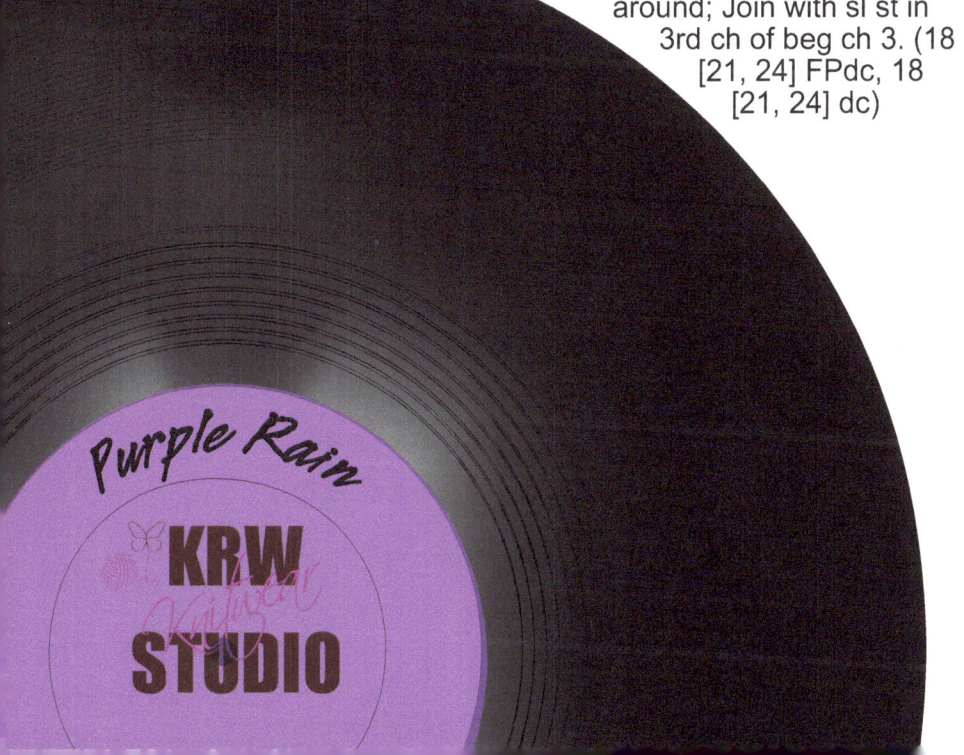

19

BAD NAME

BAD NAME

Bon Jovi is my ALL TIME FAVORITE band. Bar none! I remember the first time I heard Bon Jovi on the radio… It was late 1983 and KMEL radio out of San Francisco was a rock station back then. (Who else remembers the inflatable camel they had at events?) I was driving the carpool to school one day in my 1966 Ford Mustang and the DJ announced a new song they were going to play from a boy band from New Jersey. "Runaway" was that song, and to the rest of the carpool's dismay I fell in love right then.

29 years later, they are still my favorite band. I can truly say that I have grown up with Bon Jovi. Each album they produce seems to always fit my life at the time they release it. Of course, I am a true fan and will always tell you that I love them all, but unlike most Bon Jovi fans, Jon Bon Jovi is not my favorite member of the band! David Bryan, the keyboard player is… and he has been since 1983-84. In 2008, I got to meet David Bryan in person and have my photo taken with him! A longtime dream finally fulfilled!

The Bad Name socks were designed with the lyrics of "You Give Love a Bad Name" (*Slippery When Wet* album) in mind. The color comes directly from "blood red nails on your fingertips" in the lyrics. The knee high style of socks with the cable running up the back give you that sexy look the song imparts.

For more information about Bon Jovi, visit their website at http://www.bonjovi.com.

Skill Level:
Intermediate

Finished Size:
Small fits foot circumference up to 8.5 inches
Medium fits foot circumference up to 9.5 inches
Large fits foot circumference up to 10.5 inches
Pattern is written for size Small with [Medium, Large] in brackets.

Materials:
- Black Trillium Merilion Sock (75% Superwash Merino / 25% Nylon – 3.5 oz / 437 Yards)
- 1 Skein - Color: Better Off Red
- Size D (3.25 mm) and Size E (3.5 mm) Crochet Hooks or size needed for gauge
- Yarn Needle
- Stitch Markers

Gauge:
20 esc = 4 inches

Pattern Notes:
- To make sure socks match, work 2 socks at once.
- Do not join rounds unless otherwise indicated.
- Move up markers on each round even when not indicated.
- Mark the beginning of the round with a different color marker so that you can remember where you are.
- The Esc stitch in the foot creates a softer fabric to walk on and keeps sock from being stiff.
- Finished socks are smaller than actual fit so that they stretch to stay on the foot.

Bad Name

Directions:

Cuff:
Rnd 1: With Smaller hook, dcf 35 [39, 43] times, join with sl st to top of beg ch 3. (36 [40, 44] dcf)

NOTE: *Beg ch-3 counts as the first stitch unless otherwise noted.*

Rnd 2: Ch 3, FPdc around next dc, ✱ dc in next dc, FPdc around next dc; rep from ✱ around, join with sl st in 3rd ch of beg ch 3. (18 [20, 22] dc, 18 [20, 22] FPdc)

Rnd 3: Ch 3, FPdc around next FPdc, ✱dc in next dc, FPdc around next FPdc; rep from ✱ around, join with sl st in 3rd ch of beg ch 3. (18 [20, 22] dc, 18 [20, 22] FPdc)

Leg:
NOTES:
Mark 1st stitch of rnd now and throughout unless otherwise indicated.

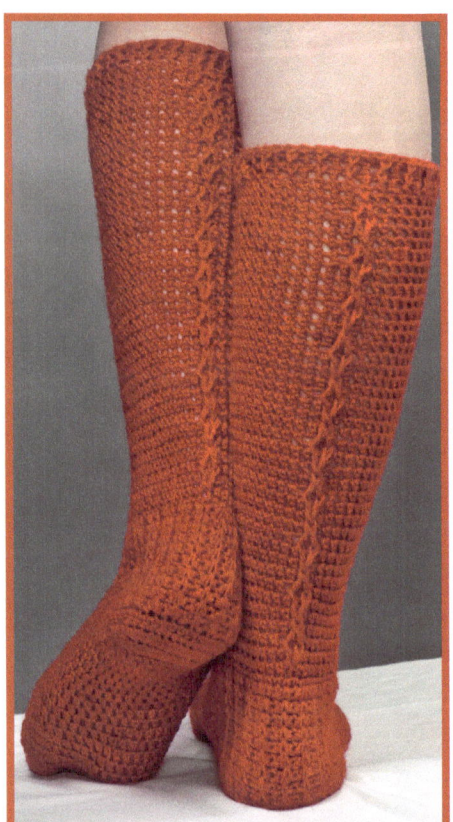

Rnd 1-2: Switching to larger hook, Esc in each st around. (36 [40, 44] Esc)

Rnd 3: Esc in first 7 [8, 9] Esc, sk next Esc, work FPdc around Esc two rows below next Esc, Esc in next Esc, work FPdc around same st as first FPdc, Esc in remaining sts around.

Rnd 4 and all even rnds: Esc in each st around. (36 [40, 44] Esc)

Rnd 5: Esc in first 8 [9, 10] esc, work CL, ESC in remaining sts around.

Rnd 7: Esc in first 7 [8, 9] Esc, sk next Esc, work FPdc around top of cluster, Esc in next Esc, work FPdc around same st as first FPdc, Esc in remaining sts around.

Rnds 8-55: Rep rnds 4-7 12 times.

Heel Flap:
NOTE: *For the Heel, you are now working in Rows instead of Rnds.*

Row 1 (RS): Evenly space 18 [20, 22] sc across, leaving the remaining ½ of the sock unworked. Ch 1, turn

Row 2: Sc in each sc across; ch 1, turn. (18 [20, 22] sc)

Row 3: Sc in first sc, ✱ sc in next sc 2 rows below, sc in next sc; rep from ✱ across, ch 1, turn.

Repeat Rows 2 and 3 until heel flap measures 2 ¾ inches (approximately 20 rows), ending with Row 2.

Heel Turn:
Row 1 (RS): Sc in next sc, sc2tog twice, sc in next 8 [10, 12] sc, sc2tog twice, sc in last sc; ch 1, turn. 14 [16, 18] sts)

Row 2: Sc in each st across; ch 1, turn.

Row 3: Sc in next sc, sc2tog twice, sc in next 4 [6, 8] sc, sc2tog twice, sc in last sc; ch 1, turn. (10 [12, 14] sts)

Row 4: Rep Row 2.

Row 5: Sc in next sc, sc2tog, sc in next 4 [6, 8] sc, sc2tog, sc in last sc; ch 1, do not turn. (8 [10, 12] sts)

Gusset:
Rnd 1 (RS): Evenly place 13 Esc along right edge of Heel Turn/Flap, PM (for gusset) in last Esc worked, Esc in each of unworked Esc, evenly space 13 Esc along left side of Heel Flap/Turn, PM (for gusset) in first Esc worked. Do not work sts along top of heel turn. (52 [56, 60] Esc around including unworked sts of heel)

NOTE: *Place unique marker in first st or rnd from this point forward unless otherwise stated.*

Rnd 2: Esc in each st to 2 st before first gusset marker, sc2tog, Esc in marked sc, Esc in each st to next marker, Esc in marked st, sc2tog, Esc in each sc to end.

Rep Rnd 2 until there are 36 [40, 44] Esc around. Remove Gusset Markers

Foot:
Rnd 1: Esc in each st around. Rep Rnd 1 until foot is 2 inches shorter than length of foot.

Toe:
Rnd 1: Sc in each sc around.

Fold Sock, making sure that the heel is centered to the back and place markers at each side edge. There should be 17 [19, 21] sts between each marker on either side. If you are not starting the next st in marked stitch, either sc to next marked st, or pull out to previous marked stitch.

Rnd 2: Sc in each sc to 2 sc before next marked sc, sc2tog, sc in marked sc, sc2tog, sc in each sc to 2 sc prior to next marker, sc2tog, sc in next marked sc, sc2tog, sc in each sc to beg of rnd marker.

Rnd 3: Sc in each sc around. Rep Rnds 2 and 3 until 20 (24, 28) sc left. Join with sl st to 1st sc. Fasten off.

Turning Sock inside out, whipstitch toe together.

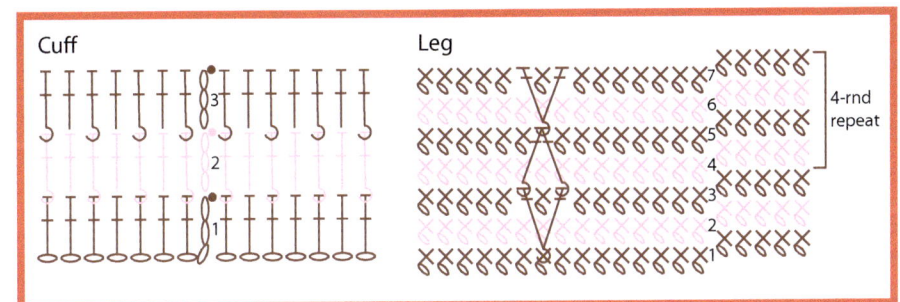

Acknowledgements

As with any book, this really wasn't a solitary endeavor! I have a lot of Thank You's to give!
First I need to thank my Yarn Dyers, Melanie Dillworth of Black Trillium Fibre Studio (http://www.etsy.com/shop/BlackTrillium) and Lorajean Kelley of Knitted Wit (http://www.etsy.com/shop/knittedwit). Honestly, I cannot say enough about how your colors have just made these socks! THANK YOU!

To my Tech Editors, Tracie Barrett and Kj Hay. Thank you for your time and effort to make not only my patterns read well, but Kj creating the faboulous charts! You both rock!

To my Model Makers Ann Chubb, Karen Taylor, Joy Prescott, Kelly Laux, Jennifer Mitton, Tracie Barrett and Jennifer Snedeker. Thank you for making my dream project come to life with your skills and talents. I could not have done it without you!

To Shannon and Jason Mullett-Bowlsby of Shibaguyz Designs (http://www.shibaguyz.com). Thank you for your creativity, skill and total craziness! (Yes, Shannon, I mean you!) This book would not be the beautiful thing it is without your talents in photography and layout. And for being two of the best friends a girl can have in this industry!

And last but definitely not least, Thank you to my family! David, Tyler and Cassie, you are the best fans a designer could ask for. Thanks for helping me pick the titles, come up with color ideas, allowing me to use your guitars and your feet in photography and just rooting me on through the whole thing! I love you <3

Special Stitches:

Double Crochet Foundation (dcf):
A.) Ch 3, YO, insert hook into 3rd ch from hook, YO and pull through st., YO, pull through one loop on hook (ch 1 made), YO, [pull through 2 loops on hook] twice (2nd dc made).

B.) kYO, insert hook into ch 1 made under first stitch, YO and pull through st., YO, pull through one loop on hook (ch 1 made), YO, [pull through 2 loops on hook] twice. Repeat from ✱ the total number of times indicated. (ch 3 at beginning counts as a stitch)

Front Post Double Crochet (FPdc): YO, insert hook from front to back to front again around the st indicated, (YO and draw through 2 loops) twice.

Extended single crochet (Esc): Insert hook in next st, YO and pull up a loop, YO and pull through one loop, YO pull through 2 loops.

Cluster (CL): kYO, insert hook from front to back around post of next FPdc, YO and pull up a loop, YO and draw through 2 loops on hook, rep from ✱ once more, YO and draw through 3 loops on hook. Sk stitch behind cluster.

Double Crochet 4 Together: (dc4tog) (Yo, insert hook in stitch indicated, YO pull up loop, YO and pull through 2 loops on hook) 4 times, YO and pull through all 5 remaining loops.

Spike Single Crochet (Ssc): Insert hook below next st 1 or more rows down (indicated thus: Ssc1, Ssc2, Ssc 3, etc), YO, pull loop through and up to height of current row, YO and draw through both loops on hook.

Bead Chain (Bch): Using smaller crochet hook, place one bead on that hook then remove loop from larger hook and place on smaller hook, slide bead so that it slips over the loop on the hook then place loop back on the larger hook; YO and pull through loop with bead on it.

Bead Double Crochet (Bdc): YO, insert the hook into stitch to be worked and pull the loop through, YO and pull through two loops; using smaller crochet hook, place one bead on hook then remove loop just made in previous step and place on smaller hook, slide bead so that it slips over the loop on the hook then place loop back on the larger hook; YO again and pull through last two The bead is to be placed in the middle of the double crochet.

Abbreviations:

Ch – Chain
Dc – Double Crochet
Dcf – Double Crochet Foundation
Esc – Extended Single Crochet

FPdc - Front Post Double Crochet
PM – Place marker
Sc – Single Crochet
Sc2Tog – Single Crochet 2 Together

Sk - Skip
St – Stitch
Sl st - Slip Stitch

Stitch Diagram Key

- • = slip stitch (sl st)
- ○ = Chain (ch)
- × = Single Crochet (sc)
- ⚹ = Extended Single Crochet (Esc)
- = Double Crochet Foundation (dcf)
- = Front Post Double Crochet (FPdc)
- = 2- FPdc Cluster (CL)
- † = Double Crochet (dc)
- ⌒ = work in back loop only
- = Double Crochet 2 Together (dc2tog)
- = Double Crochet 4 Together (dc4tog)
- = 7-dc Cluster (CL)
- = 3-dc Cluster (CL)
- = Spike Single Crochet (Ssc)

Copyright © 2012 KRW Knitwear Studio. All rights reserved.
This publication is protected under federal copyright laws. Reproduction or distribution of any part of this publication in any form including, but not limited to, print, photocopying, scanning or on the internet through posting or email is prohibited without written authorization from KRW Knitwear Studio.

www.ingramcontent.com/pod-product-compliance
Lightning Source LLC
Chambersburg PA
CBHW061402090426
42743CB00002B/116